Signatures

ASSESSMENT

EMERGENT LITERACY IN KINDERGARTEN

SENIOR AUTHORS
ROGER C. FARR
DOROTHY S. STRICKLAND

HARCOURT BRACE & COMPANY
Orlando Atlanta Austin Boston San Francisco Chicago Dallas New York
Toronto London

Printed in the United States of America

Printed in the United States of America

ISBN 0-15-307350-0

1 2 3 4 5 6 7 8 9 10 073 97 96 95

Contents

What Should Kindergarten Assessment Be?

Children's language develops quickly when they are in kindergarten. They are incessant explorers who make sense of their world by talking about it, acting things out, comparing new things with things they already understand. They write with pictures and scribbles and all sorts of invented spelling. They listen eagerly to new stories and explanations, and they learn to recognize that print represents the stories we read to them.

Getting to Know the Children

Getting to know your children is the primary and continuing challenge of assessment. This means taking a series of closer looks at each child's language development over time—his or her speaking, listening, reading, and writing. A thorough assessment program relies on kid watching, collections of work samples in portfolios, discussions with children about their work samples, and periodic assessments.

Focusing on Language

Since it is impossible to separate all that a child is from his or her language, the focus of assessment is on the whole child, with a special emphasis on language. Oral language, the primary source of a young child's emergent literacy, becomes particularly important when you are assessing kindergartners. Therefore, observations of children in natural settings that encourage interaction should be the main source of information about their growth.

Integrating and Sharing What You Learn

Information for curriculum planning is one outcome of a comprehensive, ongoing assessment program. More than this, knowledge of your children's language development is something you can share with them. Children who recognize and take pride in their emergent literacy are children who are partners with you in their own education.

Using the Kindergarten Assessment Program

To assess children's progress in kindergarten, take a minute to think about your own teaching style and about the assessment goals for kindergartens in your district.

Assessing the Group

One of your main concerns may be to know how the group is doing as a whole, particularly at the beginning of the year. In this case, you will want to do the Theme Project presentation that closes each theme in the *Teacher's Edition*. These oral and written activities will help you informally evaluate how everyone is working together.

Assessing Shared Reading

You may want to collect information about the effectiveness of the shared reading experiences you're providing for your children. If so, use the checklist for shared reading on page 21 of this booklet. You may also find useful the Informal Assessment notes that appear next to the shared reading activities throughout both volumes of the *Teacher's Edition*.

Assessing Each Child

To zero in on individual children's progress, this booklet offers you four different methods of assessment, all of which can be integrated into the natural classroom environment:

- **"Kid Watching"**
- **Portfolio Assessment**
- **Emergent Literacy Inventories**
- **Performance Assessment**

The management grid on the next page shows how to use these methods of assessment throughout the year.

Managing Your Assessment System

WHAT	WHERE TO FIND IT	WHEN	CHILD'S TASK	TEACHER'S TASK
Informal Assessment Notes	*Teacher's Edition*	Ongoing		Watches and listens for specific behaviors as children complete a task.
"Kid Watching"	*Teacher's Edition; Assessment: Emergent Literacy in Kindergarten*	Ongoing	Engages in literacy activities arising naturally in daily school activities.	Observes and records information on anecdotal record sheets or checklist or in diaries.
End-of-Theme Assessment	*Teacher's Edition*	Monthly (approx.)	Participates in a guided group activity.	Leads activity; observes groups' responses; may collect written work to include in portfolios.
Portfolio Assessment	*Assessment: Emergent Literacy in Kindergarten*	3 times a year	Selects and discusses written materials with teacher.	Discusses reading and writing with child; takes notes.
Emergent Literacy Inventories	*Assessment: Emergent Literacy in Kindergarten*	As needed during the year	Varies with type of inventory, see pages 29-34.	Varies with type of inventory, see pages 29-34.
Performance Assessment	*Assessment: Emergent Literacy in Kindergarten*	3 times a year	Listens and responds to an unfamiliar, illustrated story.	Reads story; uses a written activity to assess child's understanding of story elements.

“PUTTING THE ‘KID WATCHING’ PHILOSOPHY TO WORK IN THE KINDERGARTEN CLASSROOM INVOLVES OBSERVATION, INTERACTION, AND ANALYSIS.”

Kid Watching

KID WATCHING

ASSESSING SHARED READING AND WRITING EXPERIENCES

CHECKLISTS

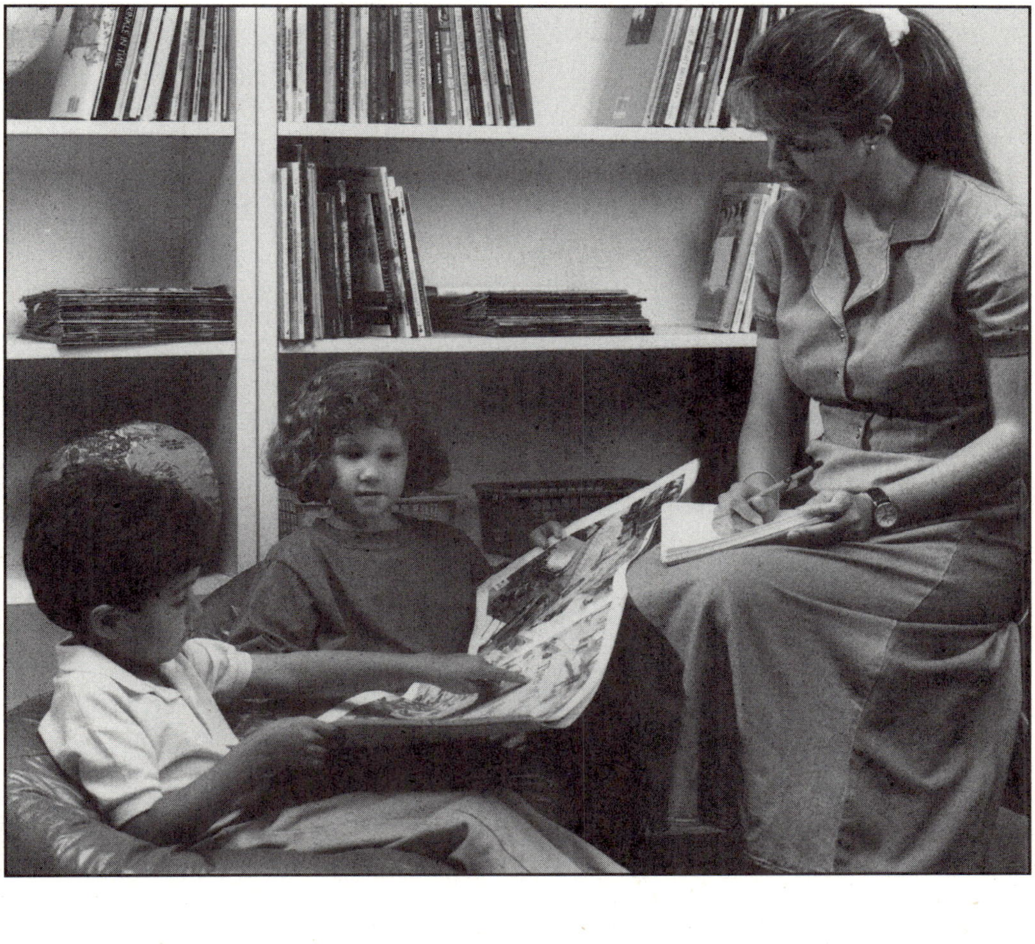

Kindergarten Assessment as "Kid Watching"

Kindergarten teachers are continually monitoring children's development. They start by establishing the emotional as well as the physical environment for learning. Within this context, they offer children many kinds of experiences. Some involve teacher-guided group instruction, such as shared reading and response to literature. Other experiences are geared more to cooperative learning and personal choice, such as center-based activities. Still other activities involve teacher and child in one-on-one instruction.

A good kindergarten program offers a balance between teacher-guided and child-centered experiences. Effective teachers know that by "kid watching" as children participate in these activities, they can build a viable profile of each child as a learner. Kid watching, the process of monitoring children's ongoing development through daily activities that are integral to instruction, is at the center of such an assessment program.

Putting the kid-watching philosophy to work in the kindergarten classroom involves observation, interaction, and analysis (Goodman, 1989, p. 8).

Observation

Observation includes the examination of what children are doing as the teacher stands on the sidelines. Very often, the teacher focuses on an individual child working independently or as a member of a group. (See the record-keeping forms on pages 8–14 of this booklet.)

Sometimes, however, the teacher may also want to watch a small group of children in action during center time. Are they making use of print in the environment? Do they seem to be applying strategies introduced during teacher-guided instruction? Are the materials in the center serving their purpose? How might the center function more effectively?

One way to streamline your note taking when observing is to jot down impressions on gummed labels. Later, put them in a child's folder or portfolio, or in your own records about center activity.

Interaction

Interaction enables a teacher to gather information during conferences about work in progress. A teacher's questions help both teacher and child discover what the child knows. (See pages 22–23.) Teacher-child dialogues about a story or a drawing, the "reading" of a favorite book, or the literacy events that occur during free-play activities yield excellent information about how well a child is using his or her emergent literacy.

Most often, these interactions will be brief encounters that take advantage of opportune or "teachable" moments. For that reason, it helps to keep note cards or other materials handy at all times for record keeping.analysis

Analysis

Analysis of literacy activities—reading stories, writing responses to a big book, inventing conversations between two homemade puppets—is an in-depth study of children's language awareness and language use. A teacher uses his or her psycholinguistic and sociolinguistic knowledge to understand where children are and what can be done to help them progress as emerging readers and writers.

Information from the three processes described above helps confirm what a teacher may already know intuitively about his or her children. Pages 6–7 describe how these kid-watching tools may be used during a shared reading or shared writing.

Reference
*Goodman, Yetta. "Evaluation of Students." In
K. S. Goodman, Y. M. Goodman, and W. Hood (Eds.).
The Whole Language Evaluation Book. Heinemann: 1989.

Assessing Shared Reading and Writing Experiences

Shared reading and writing naturally include a great deal of child/teacher interaction. What we know about first-language learning and parent/child interaction during family storybook reading tells us that shared reading helps children learn to read almost as effortlessly as they learned to talk. Similarly, during shared writing experiences children observe various writing behaviors modeled. The chart below shows how this works.

ROLES OF TEACHER AND CHILD DURING SHARED READING AND WRITING	
TEACHER	CHILD
Presents whole tasks	Experiences whole tasks
Gives active support	Gains knowledge; enjoys reading
Intervenes when needed	Internalizes textual frameworks and language patterns
Gradually releases support	Internalizes strategies
Offers opportunities for child to apply new learning	Practices strategies using whole texts in meaningful ways

Assessment during shared reading and writing

The checklists on the facing page can be used in two ways. First, they can help you monitor the overall progress of the group or the progress of specific individuals whose needs are especially challenging. Second, the checklists are reminders of the major purposes for shared reading and writing. All teachers have their favorite stories and writing forms, each one especially good for teaching a few specific skills and strategies. A checklist helps ensure that none of these concepts are missed.

Observing and analyzing

Most children really enjoy whole-group literacy experiences. When you have a child who doesn't seem to, naturally you want to know why. Is this due to a problem with learning the language? Could it be a visual or auditory problem that should be checked by a professional? Is the child shy? Or, perhaps you have a child who is functioning at a very advanced level. You may want to observe this child more closely, to determine whether he or she is ready for more challenging materials. The checklist will help you know what to look for in these individuals.

CHECKLIST FOR MONITORING SHARED READING

Children demonstrate understanding of the following concepts:

- ❍ Print contains meaning
- ❍ Pictures convey and enhance meaning
- ❍ Left-to-right direction
- ❍ Book title, author, etc.
- ❍ Words, letters, etc.
- ❍ Discuss meanings related to characters and events
- ❍ Make and confirm reasonable predictions
- ❍ Infer words in cloze activities
- ❍ Remember sequence of events

CHECKLIST FOR MONITORING SHARED WRITING

Children demonstrate the following behaviors:

- ❍ Show interest in writing
- ❍ Understand that writing has a variety of functions
- ❍ Participate in stages of the writing process
- ❍ Contribute ideas about a topic
- ❍ Voluntarily use classroom writing center
- ❍ Refer to class-composed stories, letters, charts
- ❍ View themselves as writers

Child's Name ______________________________

LISTENING

1 = no behavior

2 = beginning behavior

3 = developing behavior

4 = secure behavior

	Date	Date	Date
Distinguishes individual sounds in a word (phonemic awareness)			
Responds to simple directions, commands, and questions			
Acquires new vocabulary words			
Listens and responds to oral readings			
Listens to peers			
Focuses attention on a speaker			
Responds meaningfully in conversation			
Hears and responds to repetitive speech sounds			
Appreciates prose, poetry, and rhymes			
Listens for information			
Follows three-step oral directions			

Comments:

____

____

____

____

Child's Name____

SPEAKING

1 = no behavior

2 = beginning behavior

3 = developing behavior

4 = secure behavior

	Date	Date	Date
Uses language to satisfy personal needs (hygiene, self-help, etc.)			
Initiates conversations with teacher and with peers			
Describes objects and pictures			
Role-plays in a variety of situations (alone or with others)			
Retells stories and repeats songs			
Is aware of appropriate speaking behavior and voice volume			
Relates ideas in a logical order			
Shares facts and information			
Asks relevant questions in a variety of situations			
Reads aloud			

Comments:

____

____

____

____

Child's Name ______________________________

READING

1 = no behavior

2 = beginning behavior

3 = developing behavior

4 = secure behavior

	Date	Date	Date
Recognizes environmental print			
Recognizes own name in print			
Enjoys listening to stories			
Participates in shared reading activities			
Voluntarily looks at books			
Handles a book correctly (holds right side up, turns pages, etc.)			
Recalls details from familiar stories			
Retells stories in a logical order			
Uses pictures to gain meaning from text			
Responds to stories through interpretive activities (art, drama, etc.)			
Recognizes that print contains meaning			
Recognizes common or important words in stories			
Retells own stories			

Comments:

____

____

Child's Name ____________________

AUDITORY AND VISUAL AWARENESS

1 = no behavior

2 = beginning behavior

3 = developing behavior

4 = secure behavior

	Date	Date	Date
Identifies rhyming words			
Recognizes letter names			
Matches capital and lowercase letters			
Matches repeated words in stories			
Identifies word boundaries			
Discriminates between beginning sounds			
Matches beginning sounds			
Practices phonemic segmentation			
Associates beginning sounds with corresponding consonants			
Recognizes word family patterns			

Comments:

____

____

____

____

Child's Name____

WRITING

1 = no behavior

2 = beginning behavior

3 = developing behavior

4 = secure behavior

	Date	Date	Date
Voluntarily writes			
Participates in shared writing— narrative, functional, informational			
Draws pictures and tells stories about them			
Writes own name			
Dictates captions or stories about pictures			
Uses personal experiences as source of ideas for writing			
Enjoys sharing compositions with peers			
Records information			
Asks how to spell words			

Comments:

____

____

____

____

Child's Name________________________________

WRITING CONVENTIONS

1 = no behavior

2 = beginning behavior

3 = developing behavior

4 = secure behavior

	Date	Date	Date
Prints symbols horizontally, from left to right			
Uses mostly scribble writing			
Uses mostly letter strings or random letters			
Often uses a single letter to represent a whole word			
Uses temporary spelling to write words			
Leaves spaces between words			
Uses some vowels in spelling			
Makes transition between temporary spelling and conventional spelling			
Shows awareness of how to use capital and lowercase forms			
Begins to use punctuation			

Comments:

____

____

____

Child's Name ____________________

THINKING

1 = no behavior

2 = beginning behavior

3 = developing behavior

4 = secure behavior

	Date	Date	Date
Uses all senses to observe environment			
Builds on prior knowledge			
Sequences events and stories			
Recognizes cause and effect			
Classifies/categorizes			
Distinguishes between real and make-believe			
Predicts outcomes			
Draws reasonable conclusions			
Interprets viewpoints and feelings			

Comments:

____

____

____

____

> "EVALUATION IS NOT SOMETHING THAT IS DONE *TO* CHILDREN, BUT RATHER ***FOR*** AND ***BY*** CHILDREN."

Portfolio Assessment

USING PORTFOLIOS

GETTING STARTED

CONDUCTING PORTFOLIO CONFERENCES

EVALUATING PORTFOLIOS

EVALUATION CHECKLISTS

Using Portfolios with Kindergarten Children

Portfolio assessment is child-centered, contributing to an environment where learning flourishes. Using portfolios, children share collections of their work and interact with others to discuss it. As an outcome, children gain confidence in themselves and in their abilities.

What Are Portfolios?

Portfolios can be many different things and can be used in many different ways. Physically, a portfolio can be a folder, a box, or space on a shelf. The one physical element that portfolios have in common is that they are places or containers in which children's work is collected. Portfolios can include work samples in the form of finished products, first drafts, notes, lists, and pictures.

A portfolio system is based on the belief that portfolios should help children take ownership of their own literacy development. Portfolios can also provide teachers with a more comprehensive basis on which to judge children's progress than can traditional tests. Integrated reading and writing portfolios

• are an integral part of the total reading/writing program.

• provide many opportunities for children to show what they can do and what they are proud of.

• provide a focus for child-teacher and child-child discussions about reading and writing ideas and interests.

• give children a sense of control over their own literacy development.

• serve as a springboard to more reading and writing activities. include finished and unfinished work, pictures, and lists of writing ideas.

• are an effective instructional tool and not merely another way to evaluate children's reading and writing.

Why Should Portfolios Be Used?

Using portfolios is not a new idea. Indeed, teachers have always collected samples of children's work, discussed with children their favorite books and stories, and talked with them about their writing.

For children, the portfolio system

• enhances self-esteem because portfolios emphasize what they *can* do.

•provides an opportunity for them to be responsible for their own learning as they reflect on their reading and writing.

•is noncompetitive because each child's portfolio reflects his or her unique development.

For teachers, the portfolio system

•provides regular opportunities to talk with children about their literacy development and about their reading and writing interests and attitudes.

•provides a method of continual informal assessment for the purpose of instructional planning.

What Does a Portfolio System Look Like?

For children, part of the fun of portfolios is making their own. Here are some classroom-tested ideas you can choose from:

Each child decorates his or her own folder.

Each child uses a shopping bag to store materials.

Each child decorates his or her own shoe box.

Each child has his or her own space on a shelf.

Children's portfolios should be readily accessible to them so that they can add materials, work on unfinished pictures and stories, and share with other children what they've done. You will begin to realize that these portfolios are not merely storage places for keeping children's finished or best work, but are working portfolios that help children take responsibility for their ongoing progress.

Regularly scheduled teacher-child conferences are an important component of a portfolio system. Since kindergartners' abilities and interests vary widely, a conference with one child may consist of talking about pictures he or she has drawn, while another child may want to read a book he or she has written and illustrated. Frequent impromptu conferences to discuss particular works in progress are also part of a portfolio system.

A teacher reviews children's portfolios to plan instruction, to write reports to family members, to prepare for parent-teacher conferences, and to evaluate the progress being made by individual children and by the group as a whole.

How Can a Portfolio System Be Managed?

Keeping track of all the reading and writing children do, helping children collect work to keep in their portfolios, and reviewing the contents of portfolios might, at first, seem like an impossible management task for teachers. However, it needn't be difficult at all. If you use portfolios as part of your ongoing reading/language arts program, you will find that they actually lessen your work and help you better organize your instruction. The most important factor in using portfolios is to remember that the portfolios belong to the children—ownership of and pride in their work is key.

"PORTFOLIOS SHOULD BE A NORMAL PART OF YOUR CLASSROOM ROUTINE."

Getting Started

Individualize your portfolio system to suit the children and your classroom. Just as no two children are alike, neither are any two classrooms alike.

Follow these suggestions to start a successful portfolio system:

- **Portfolios should be a normal part of your classroom routine.** Talk with children about the use of the portfolios. Emphasize that their portfolios are special places in which to keep their reading and writing work. You may also want to talk about professionals who keep portfolios of their work, such as artists and photographers.

- **Children need to feel a sense of ownership of their portfolios.** Encourage them to decorate their portfolios. They may want to paste or draw favorite story characters on the covers. Children should write their names on their portfolios.

- **Portfolios should be easily accessible to children.** Portfolios should be kept in a place in the classroom where children can find them easily and use them daily. They will be adding their stories and reports, lists of books and stories they've read, and their ideas about reading and writing.

Tip: Share your own writing!
If you, too, keep a reading/writing portfolio, you may find that showing it to the children from time to time provides them with a helpful model.

Tip: Promote ownership!
Comment on the individuality and creativity children show in their work so that they understand that you recognize the portfolios as their property.

- **Be sure that children understand that the portfolios are their responsibility.**

One of the most important features of any portfolio system is that children become actively involved in their own literacy development. Most kindergarten children believe in themselves as writers, with something important to say, and they are eager to show off their work. You can further encourage children in portfolio conferences by asking them about other books they have read and other writing they have done. Children who are reluctant to write will probably benefit from cooperative writing activities with a partner or a small group.

Tip:

Make portfolio conferences work both for you and for children

Some children may become distracted if you take notes during the conference. Threfore, you may want to make your notes afterwards. If you take notes during a conference, tell teh child waht you're writing to help him or her feel more comfortable.

- **Don't make the portfolios a testing program.**

Portfolio conferences are a time for you and a child to discuss his or her reading and writing ideas, interests, and development. Don't use them as a time to grade children. Your objective is to find out what children like to read and write about, how they feel about their own reading and writing, and what they think they need to do to become better readers and writers.

Tip:

Make portfolios accessible!

Don't keep portfolios in a file drawer to be used by children only when you feel they are needed.

Tip:

Make children's portfolios important

If you make portfolios an integral part of your classroom routine, children will use them not just to store their work but to get fresh writing ideas, to have something to share with classmates, and to learn more about themselves as emergent readers and writers.

- **During portfolio conferences, you will learn a great deal about children and their developing reading and writing interests and abilities.**

The portfolio conference should be a time for a child to show off his or her favorite piece of writing, to discuss a favorite book or story, or to talk about things that he or she would like to read and write about. Through these discussions, you will learn far more about the child than you could ever learn from a formal test.

- **Portfolio conferences are essential to the success of a portfolio program.**

Conferencing—discussions of children's reading and writing activities—makes the portfolio system a rich and vital activity. When children talk about their reading and writing, they think about the ideas that interest them most, about why they liked certain selections, and about how they can make their literacy efforts even more successful. Discussion is based on reflection, and reflection leads to an understanding of how one is becoming literate.

Tip: **Be flexible!**

Conferences may also involve two or more children; a child and his or her family members; you and a child's family members; or you and an administrator.

Tip: **Reluctant writers may blossom if you write down their dictated stories!**

A really reluctant writer may not have much to share during a portfolio conference. Your time may be well spent writing down a story he or she wants to tell, either before or after the child has drawn pictures to go with the story. Be sure to read the story aloud after he or she has finished dictating it.

Tip: **Make yourself available to children**

Post an appointment sheet so that children can sign up anytime for private portfolio discussion time with you. You'll be surprised how many children want to tell you about their reading and writing between your regularly scheduled conferences.

Tip: **Let children collaborate!**

Try a partner approach in getting the portfolios started. You will save time and help children become collaborative learners.

“ASK QUESTIONS THAT OPEN UP CONVERSATIONS RATHER THAN SHUT DOWN COMMUNICATION.”

Conducting Portfolio Conferences

Conferences should be a regular part of your reading/language arts program. You should hold an individual conference with each child at least three times a year. The time for conferences should be carefully planned.

What Are the Essentials of a Conference?

Conferences are really quite simple. All you have to do is remember that a conference is a time for sharing and that you are having a conversation with a person who has much to offer. Here are some guidelines:

1. Allow the child to do most of the talking. You will learn much more about the child if you let him or her talk.

2. Avoid being evaluative. Respect the child as a learner. If you think of the conference as a time for the child to reflect on his or her own reading and writing, you will be less likely to be judgmental.

3. Avoid interruptions. Children need our undivided attention during a conference. If you are constantly interrupted, the child will be unable to develop his or her ideas. Also, if you allow constant interruptions, the child may conclude that this one-to-one discussion is not very important to you.

4. Ask questions that open up conversations rather than shut down communication. Use open-ended questions that ask for explanations, expansions, examples, and discussion. You learn more about children when they explain, justify, clarify, and express their ideas and beliefs. The quality of the responses will depend on the quality of the questions you ask. Children will provide more explanations if they believe that you are interested in and truly respect them and their opinions.

5. Use the conference as a time to plan goals with the child. Ask questions like What do you plan to read or write about next? What are you planning to do with this story? How can I help you?

6. Write notes about what you have learned. Take time after each conference to jot down notes about the conference and the goals you and the child have discussed. Add the notes to the child's portfolio so that they can be reviewed at the next conference.

Child's Name________________________________ Date__________________

CONFERENCE CHECKLIST

- ❍ is willing to share ideas
- ❍ shows confidence and risk-taking in experimenting with new ideas
- ❍ uses information from other models, for example, from other authors and genres or from friends
- ❍ explores personal interests through reading and writing
- ❍ is aware of audience
- ❍ gives evidence of how feedback from others has been incorporated into reading and writing
- ❍ uses expressive language in discussing a previously read book or a selected piece of writing

GENERAL QUESTION/STATEMENT	FOLLOW-UP QUESTIONS
1. Tell me how you use your portfolio.	Why did you organize your portfolio this way? How did you decide which pieces to include in your portfolio?
2. Tell me about one story in your portfolio.	Why is this story important to you? Why did you choose to write this? Where did you get the idea? Would you like to read it to me? Did you have any problems writing it?
3. Tell me about a book that you have read.	Explain to me why this book is important to you. Why did you decide to read this book? Why would someone else like reading it?
4. What are you going to read and write next?	How can I help you with this? What will you do first? Is there someone with whom you would like to work?

Evaluating Portfolios

Portfolio evaluation or assessment of a child's work is an ongoing process. In addition to the content of the work presented in the portfolios, important information can be gathered through discussions with each child. These discussions can be summarized quickly and accurately on kid-watching checklists.

How Can Portfolios Be Used Effectively to Assess a Child's Progress?

You can use portfolios daily to learn about children and about their developing reading and writing skills. Here are some important points to keep in mind when you use the contents of a portfolio as part of your assessment:

• The goal of the assessment is to learn what children read and write, what their reading and writing interests are, and how you can help them become better readers and writers.

• Evaluation is not something that is done *to* children, but rather *for* and *by* children. The emphasis is on helping children see all the things they can do well. Children should feel a sense of accomplishment, not defeat, when they discuss their reading and writing.

• Portfolio assessment should bring together reading, writing, listening, and speaking, and children's use of portfolios should help them see the connections. The portfolio system gives you an opportunity to see a child's total reading/language arts development because each child's portfolio includes work produced from a variety of integrated reading and writing activities. In addition, as you conduct child-teacher conferences, you can note each child's listening and speaking skills.

Process Evaluation

Process evaluation, determining how someone accomplishes a task, should be the central focus of the child-teacher conferences. The discussions will help both you and the child learn about the processes he or she is using in reading and writing.

Questions that you ask during portfolio conferences will be helpful in getting children to reflect on their reading and writing. When children think about how they want to organize their portfolios before a conference, they review their work and get a sense of what they have been reading and writing.

The information gathered during the conferences forms the basis for setting specific reading and writing goals for individuals and for the group as a whole. The conferences also provide opportunities for you to advise children about the skills, strategies, and activities that will help them become more effective users of language.

Product Evaluation

Product evaluation assesses how well someone has accomplished a task. Usually the reviews are conducted at the end of a semester or at the end of the school year. However, you may find it useful to sum up a child's progress just before a conference with a family member or a school administrator. Three dimensions of a child's portfolio that need to be evaluated are

- the amount of reading and writing the child has been doing.
- the child's general attitudes toward reading and writing as well as the specific topics and genres the child enjoys.
- the child's use of reading and writing strategies.

In What Ways Can Information from Evaluations Be Used to Enhance Instruction?

There is no question that the more children read and write, the better readers and writers they become. Of course, improvement also depends on the effort and interest they invest in their work and on the topics they read and write about.

If you are going to encourage children to read and write more, find out what topics interest them. Does a particular child always read animal stories? Does another read the same stories over and over? Do some children shun poetry? All this information can come from children's portfolios. Your instruction should build on these interests and attitudes.

Finally, you want to know whether your children are growing in their use of the strategies that will make them more effective as readers and writers. Are they attempting new writing forms? Do they take risks with language? Are they becoming more reflective about their reading? Samples from their portfolios and information from conferences will tell you this.

BASIC STEPS FOR EVALUATING A PORTFOLIO

Step 1:

Review the child's reading and writing.

By starting with a review of the volume of a child's work for a particular evaluation period, you will become generally familiar with what the child has been reading and writing for that period. You will also want to review the notes that you made during your portfolio conferences.

An evaluation of the amount of reading and writing is a subjective judgment. Remember that what is outstanding for one child may be average for another. Your goal should be to evaluate each child's progress over time.

Step 2:

Review the child's interests and attitudes.

After reviewing the reading and writing the child has been doing, you will be ready to consider the child's attitude toward reading and writing. You will find that some children include a wide variety of reading and writing materials in their portfolios, while others include only a limited range. One of your goals will be to help the child broaden his or her literacy activities.

It is important to use the portfolio as a primary source of evidence of the child's attitudes and interests. If you base your evaluation only on other classroom behaviors, you may misjudge a child who is in fact an eager reader and writer but who doesn't outwardly show enthusiasm during class.

Step 3:

Review the child's use of reading/writing strategies.

The most important goal in teaching reading and writing is to help children develop effective strategies. As you review the child's use of reading/writing strategies, make sure that you carefully examine

- the child's work produced during theme projects and in various centers.
- the child's comments about his or her own reading and writing. The child's reflections can help you determine how he or she is progressing as a reader and writer and which strategies are and are not being used.
- the child's reactions to what has been read. A child's comments often give insight into his or her developing interests and reading strategies. For example, you can note whether a child relates what has been read to personal experiences.

REVIEW OF PORTFOLIO READING MATERIALS

Child's Name______________________________

Teacher's Name______________________________

Date__________________ Grade__________ School__________________

1 = Limited 2 = Below expectation 3 = Average 4 = Above expectation 5 = Outstanding

Assessment	1	2	3	4	5	Teacher Comments
Emergent reading skills						
Recognizes speech/print relationship						
Understands concepts of letters/words						
Handles books appropriately						
Attitudes toward reading						
Chooses reading during free time						
Reads many books/stories						
Listens attentively to stories						
Reading interests						
Has favorite books/stories						
Retells familiar stories						
Participates in discussions about books/stories						
Reading skills/strategies						
Constructs meaning when reading						
Relates stories to background						
Shows confidence as a reader						

SUMMARY ASSESSMENT

	For This Review			Since Last Reviewed		
Assessment	Outstanding	Average	Limited	Improving	About the Same	Seems Poorer
Amount of reading						
Attitudes toward reading						
Reading skills/strategies						

REVIEW OF PORTFOLIO WRITING MATERIALS

Child's Name______________________________

Teacher's Name______________________________

Date______________ Grade__________ School______________________

1 = Limited 2 = Below expectation 3 = Average 4 = Above expectation 5 = Outstanding

Assessment	1	2	3	4	5	Teacher Comments
Emergent writing skills						
Draws to convey meaning						
Writes letterlike shapes and random letters						
Discusses drawing/writing						
Copies letters/words						
Attitudes toward writing						
Shows enthusiasm for writing						
Combines drawing and writing						
Writing Skills						
Participates in prewriting activities						
Writes for specific audiences						
Focuses on meaning						
Mechanics						
Demonstrates knowledge of sound/ symbol correspondence						
Uses appropriate spacing between words						
Writes left to right						

SUMMARY ASSESSMENT

	For This Review			Since Last Reviewed		
Assessment	Outstanding	Average	Limited	Improving	About the Same	Seems Poorer
Amount of writing and drawing						
Attitudes toward writing and drawing						
Quality of writing						

“ SYSTEMATIC, REGULAR ASSESSMENT FOR EACH CHILD IS THE GOAL. ”

Emergent Literacy Inventories

USING THE INVENTORIES

PHONEMIC AWARENESS INTERVIEW

INVENTORY OF CONCEPTS ABOUT PRINT

INVENTORY OF CONCEPTS ABOUT EMERGENT READING

CAPITAL/LOWERCASE LETTER INVENTORY

MATCHING BEGINNING SOUNDS INVENTORY

Using The Inventories

THE PHONEMIC AWARENESS INTERVIEW (pages 35-37)

Phonemic awareness is an understanding that speech is composed of a series of individual sounds (phonemes). A child who demonstrates an ability to orally manipulate phonemes is likely to be successful in reading. Children who have difficulty attending to and manipulating the sounds in their language are likely to have problems learning to read. These children need additional experience with oral language play to heighten their sensitivity to the phonemic basis of speech.

The Phonemic Awareness Interview is an oral test designed to provide information about a child's level of phonemic awareness to help the teacher plan literacy activities. The Interview consists of four tasks, each one measuring a different aspect of phonemic awareness: 1) sound matching, 2) sound isolation, 3) sound blending, and 4) sound segmenting. The tasks are sequenced from the easiest to the most difficult. You may use any one, or all, of the tasks to assess each child. A model, a sample item, and test items are provided for each task. As the child responds orally to each item, record the child's responses on the recording form.

General Testing Considerations

Administer the Interview individually in a quiet and comfortable setting. This will help ensure that the child attends to the task and can give the teacher insights into problems the child may be having.

There is no time limit; however, a period of 15–20 minutes is suggested. It is recommended that all tasks be administered in a single session, but they can be given separately over several days if necessary.

Become familiar with the directions and test items. The text in bold type is intended to be read aloud. The other information is for the teacher only and should not be read aloud. However, you should feel free to rephrase the directions, to repeat the sample, or to give additional examples to make sure the child understands what to do.

You and the child should be seated at a flat table or desk. The best seating location for you is facing the child, to facilitate clear diction and immediate recording. Before beginning an Interview, spend a few minutes in light, friendly conversation with the child. Don't refer to the Interview as a "test." Tell the child you would like to play some "word games."

Specific Testing Considerations

Follow these steps for a Phonemic Awareness Interview:

1. Duplicate a copy of the "Phonemic Awareness Interview Administering/Recording Form" for each task and one "Summary of Performance Form" for each child. You will record a child's responses on the "Administering/Recording Form" and the totals on the "Summary of Performance Form." The child will not need any materials.

2. Explain that the words the child hears and says every day are made up of sounds and that you will be saying some words and sounds and asking questions about them. It will be helpful to the child if you accentuate each word, syllable, or phoneme by prolonging and pausing between words and sounds.

3. Begin the Interview with Task 1, Sound Matching, and proceed through Task 4, Sound Segmenting. If the child has difficulty with the first few items or cannot answer them, you may wish to discontinue conducting the Interview until a later time. If the child misses half of the items at any task, move on to the next task.

4. After the Interview, record the child's scores on the "Summary of Performance Form." Use the scale in the box to determine the level that best describes the child's understanding of phonemic awareness. Children whose scores reflect minimal or limited understanding may need additional oral language experiences. Several literature-based activities are provided on pages R5-8 in both volumes of the *Teacher's Edition*. You may also wish to indicate specific observations from the activity, especially those areas where the child had obvious difficulty with the task or required additional prompting.

THE INVENTORY OF CONCEPTS ABOUT PRINT AND EMERGENT READING (pages 38-39)

Suggestions for Administering

Each child should be assessed individually about three times during the kindergarten year. September/October, December/January, and April/May are suggested times. Since this is an individual assessment, it is not necessary for all children to be assessed during the same week or specific time period. Systematic, regular assessment for each child is the goal.

Using the Results

Use the checklists, along with other anecdotal records and portfolio samples, to assemble a reading/writing profile of each child. At parent/teacher conferences, use all the information you have compiled to

- emphasize what the child can do.
- explain your short- and long-term goals for the child.
- help family members understand your reading/language arts program.
- make suggestions for things family members can do at home with the child.

References

Clay, M. The Early Detection of Reading Difficulties. Portsmouth, NH: Heinemann Educational, 1979.

Sulzby, E. "Children's Emergent Reading of Favorite Storybooks: A Developmental Study." Reading Research Quarterly, 20, 451–458, 1985.

CAPITAL/LOWERCASE LETTER INVENTORY (pages 40-48)

General Testing Considerations

You may wish to use this inventory at the beginning of the year to assess children's general awareness of letter forms. The results will help you plan curriculum and match activities with children's level of familiarity with letters.

Conduct another inventory toward the end of the year to assess how well each child can match capital and lowercase letters. Children having difficulty recognizing specific letters may need additional practice with those letters. See the Phonics Workshops throughout the *Teacher's Edition*, as well as Learning Through the Literature lessons for specific letters.

Specific Testing Considerations

Tell children to find the sample box with the star at the top of the page 40. **Say: Look at the first letter in the box. It is a capital *F*. Does everyone see the capital *F*?** Pause; allow time for children to find the letter. **Then say: Now look at the other three letters in that row. Find the lowercase f.** Pause; allow time for children to look at each letter. Call on a child to supply the correct answer. **Then say: Yes, the last letter is a lowercase *f*. The lowercase *f* matches the capital *F*. So fill in the last answer circle under the lowercase *f*.**

Check to be sure children have filled in the correct answer circle, and help anyone who has difficulty. **Then say: Now put your pencils on the number 1. Look at the first letter in that row. Find the letter that is the capital form of the letter. Fill in the answer circle under it.**

Pause while children mark their answers. **Say: Does everyone understand what to do? You will see a letter at the beginning of each row. If it is a capital letter, you will find the matching lowercase letter. If the first letter in the row is a lowercase letter, you will find the matching capital letter. When you find the matching letter, fill in the answer circle under the letter, and go on to the next row. Keep working until you come to the word *Stop*! When you come to the word *Stop*!, put your pencils down and sit quietly until everyone has finished.**

MATCHING BEGINNING SOUNDS INVENTORY (pages 49-58)

General Testing Considerations

You may wish to use Part A of this inventory after the middle of the year as a practice test to help children become familiar and comfortable with standardized testing procedures. Part A includes all consonants taught in Volume 1 of the *Teacher's Edition*.

Use Part B toward the end of the year to assess children's ability to match beginning sounds. Part B includes all consonants except Q and X. Children having difficulty hearing and matching specific initial sounds may benefit from activities in the Phonics Workshops throughout the *Teacher's Edition*, as well as from the Learning Through the Literature lessons for specific letters.

Part A

Tell children to find the box with the hat at the top of the page. **Say: You see a picture of a *hat*. Listen to the word *hat*. Find the picture that begins with the same sound that you hear at the beginning of the word *hat*. You see pictures of a desk, a house, and a tent.** Pause; allow time for children to look at each picture. Call on a child to supply the correct answer. **Then say: Yes, the word *house* begins with the same sound that you hear at the beginning of the word hat. So fill in the answer circle under the *house*.**

Make sure that children have filled in the correct answer circle, and help anyone who has difficulty. **Then say: Now put your pencils on the picture of the book (row 1). Listen to the word *book*. Find the picture that begins with the same sound that you hear at the beginning of *book*. You see pictures of a mouse, a pig, and a bell. Fill in the answer circle under the picture that begins with the same sound as *book*.**

Pause while children mark their answers. Continue the test following the same procedure.

STIMULUS WORD	PICTURE NAMES
2. milk	feather, cat, moon
3. car	cup, dog, tent
4. puppet	duck, wagon, pie
5. fence	bee, fox, cat
6. sun	van, sock, door
7. hat	heart, rake, umbrella
8. boy	yarn, jet, book
9. tiger	toothbrush, house, leaf
10. mitten	horn, mouse, jar
11. pig	pencil, fan, cow
12. button	hat, girl, balloon
13. sandwich	ball, seal, fish
14. hammer	top, helicopter, king
15. tent	tiger, duck, pencil
16. cat	window, car, yo-yo
17. deer	robot, dog, fish
18. sock	nest, yarn, sun
19. mouse	horse, bear, mop
20. dinosaur	hat, doll, gate

Part B

Tell children to find the box with the tiger at the top of the page. **Say: You see a picture of a tiger. Listen to the word *tiger*. Find the picture that begins with the same sound that you hear at the beginning of the word *tiger*. You see pictures of a dog, a wagon, and a top.** Pause; allow time for children to look at each picture. Call on a child to supply the correct answer. **Then say: Yes, the word *top* begins with the same sound that you hear at the beginning of the word *tiger*. So fill in the answer circle under the *top*.**

Make sure that children have filled in the correct answer circle, and help anyone who has difficulty. **Then say: Now put your pencils on the picture of the nine** (row 21). **Listen to the word *nine*. Find the picture that begins with the same sound that you hear at the beginning of *nine*. You see pictures of a necklace, a book, and a goat. Fill in the answer circle under the picture that begins with the same sound as *nine*.**

	STIMULUS WORD	PICTURE NAMES
22.	pen	desk, pan, moon
23.	nut	nail, tiger, bus
24.	rope	rake, cat, dog
25.	sun	tent, soap, book
26.	turtle	duck, horse, table
27.	vegetables	shoe, vest, king
28.	web	house, umbrella, watch
29.	yarn	leaf, guitar, yo-yo
30.	zipper	car, zebra, hat
31.	bee	vest, pig, ball
32.	car	cage, pencil, hammer
33.	deer	house, dog, apple
34.	fan	desk, fork, bear
35.	guitar	girl, book, octopus
36.	horse	kitten, heart, violin
37.	jacks	igloo, jet, cup
38.	kangaroo	keys, soap, tent
39.	lion	lock, envelope, saw
40.	milk	ax, moon, book

Phonemic Awareness Interview Administering/Recording Form

Task 1: SOUND MATCHING

Task: The child will listen to two words and will indicate if the two words do or do not begin with the same sound.

Model: I am going to say two words. Listen carefully so you can tell me if the two words begin with the same sound. *Monkey, mother.* Listen again: *monkey, mother.* The words begin with the same sound. *Monkey* and *mother* begin with the same sound.

Sample: Listen to these two words: *rain, snow.*
Listen again: *rain, snow.*

Child's name ______________________

Date ______________________

Circle child's response.
(Correct response is in bold type.)

leg, lunch	**Same**	Different
duck, pan	Same	**Different**
sun, moon	Same	**Different**
fork, fish	**Same**	Different
chocolate, checkers	**Same**	Different
phone, poem	Same	**Different**
ball, banana	**Same**	Different
red, nut	Same	**Different**
	_____/4	_______/4

Score_________/8

Task 2: SOUND ISOLATION

Task: The child will listen to a word and then will produce the initial phoneme in the word.

Model: I am going to say a word. Then I am going to say just the beginning sound. Listen carefully for the beginning sound: *pig*. The beginning sound is /p/.

Sample: Listen to another word. This time you tell me the beginning sound. Listen carefully: goat. What is the beginning sound in goat? (/g/) You're correct. /g/ is the beginning sound in goat. (Note: If the child tells you a letter name, remind the child to tell you the sound.)

Now listen to some more words. Tell me the beginning sound you hear in each word.

Child's name ______________________

Date ______________________

	Correct Response	Child's Response
dot	/d/	____________
map	/m/	____________
sad	/s/	____________
talk	/t/	____________
cow	/k/	____________
bird	/b/	____________

Score__________/6

Task 3: SOUND BLENDING

Task: The child will listen to word sounds and will blend the sounds together to say the word.

Model: **I am going to say some sounds. Then I want you to put the sounds together to make a word. I will do the first one. Listen to the sounds: /r/-/u/-/n/. When I put the sounds /r/-/u/-/n/ together, they make the word *run*.**

Sample: Listen to these sounds: /k/-/a/-/t/. What word do you make when you put /k/-/a/-/t/ together? (cat). You're correct. /k/-/a/-/t/ makes the word *cat*. Now listen again. I will say some sounds. You put the sounds together to make a word and tell me the word.

Child's name ______________________

Date ______________________

	Correct Response	Child's Response
/g/-/o/	go	____________
/sh/-/ee/-/p/	sheep	____________
/j/-/u/-/m/-/p/	jump	____________
/a/-/n/-/t/	ant	____________
/h/-/o/-/t/	hot	____________
/l/-/i/-/p/	lip	____________
/d/-/e/-/s/-/k/	desk	____________
/b/-/i/	by	____________

Score ____________/8

Task 4: SOUND SEGMENTING

Task: The child will listen to a word and then will produce each phoneme in the word separately.

Model: **I am going to say a word. Then I am going to say each sound in the word. Listen carefully for each sound. The word is go. The sounds in go are /g/-/o/. (Be sure to articulate each sound separately. Do not simply stretch out the word.)**

Sample: Listen to this word. This time you tell me the sounds in the word. Listen carefully: *man*. What sounds do you hear in *man*? (/m/-/a/-/n/) You are correct. The sounds in the word *man* are /m/-/a/-/n/.

Now listen to some more words. Tell me the sounds you hear in these words.

Child's name ______________________

Date ______________________

	Correct Response	Child's Response
dog	/d/-/o/-/g/	____________
keep	/k/-/ee/-/p/	____________
no	/n/-/o/	____________
that	/th/-/a/-/t/	____________
me	/m/-/e/	____________
do	/d/-/oo/	____________
race	/r/-/a/-/s/	____________
in	/i/-/n/	____________

Score ____________/8

Summary of Performance Form

Phonemic Awareness Interview

Child's Name____________________ Grade ________ Date ________

Understanding of Concept

0-10 = Minimal

11-20 = Limited

21-30 = Good

Child's Score:

Sound Matching ________ /8 Comments:____________________

Sound Isolation ________ /6 Comments:____________________

Sound Blending ________ /8 Comments:____________________

Sound Segmenting ________ /8 Comments:____________________

Total ________/ 30 **Understanding of Phonemic Awareness** ____________

Comments:____

Inventory of Concepts About Print

Name__________________________**Teacher**____________________

Write in the date that the child demonstrates knowledge or control of the item.

Example: 9/22 Author's name

On the table, put a book that is familiar to the child. Ask him or her to pick it up and show you the items below. **Example: "Show me the front cover. Now, show me the back cover."**

___ Front cover　　___ Back cover

___ Title/Name of story　　___ Author's name

Open to a page with some print and ask the child to show you each of the following:

___ Top of page　　___ Bottom of page

___ A word　　___ A letter

___ A capital letter　　___ A lowercase letter

Say, "Where does it tell the reader what to say?"

"Show me where the print starts and ends."

___ Understands that print holds the message

___ Turns pages from front to back

___ Knows correct directional movement (left to right)

On a card, print a word that is repeated often in the book and show the card to the child. **Say, "Show me this word on a page in the book."**

____ Recognizes similarities in words

Inventory of Emergent Reading

DIRECTIONS: Place in front of the child three books that are familiar to him or her. Choose books with a story line rather than ABC or other basic concept books. Ask the child to select one of the books. Explain that he or she is to start at the beginning and read it to you as well as he or she can. Using the chart below, enter today's date next to the stage of emergent reading that best describes the child's rendering of the story. The same chart may be reused for each assessment.

Name______________________________ **Teacher**____________________

	DATE	DATE	DATE
Picture-governed, story not formed (Child reads by labeling and commenting on pictures. Little or no evidence of connected story line.)			
Picture-governed, oral language used (Child focuses on pictures and uses an oral language style in narration. May tell an interesting story, but language is unlike that of book.)			
Picture-governed, more written language used (Child alternates between oral language style and "reading intonation" and wording that sounds like written language. At times, rendering might sound very much like written language of book.)			
Print-governed (Child reads text in conventional manner.)			

Name________________________________

Capital/Lowercase Letter Inventory

Sample				
★	F	t ○	B ○	f ○
1	z	N ○	w ○	Z ○
2	a	A ○	n ○	B ○
3	Y	y ○	T ○	c ○
4	b	D ○	B ○	f ○
5	X	C ○	x ○	Q ○

Go on.

6	c	C ○	Z ○	t ○
7	W	s ○	w ○	N ○
8	d	F ○	b ○	D ○
9	V	W ○	r ○	v ○
10	e	g ○	E ○	a ○
11	U	L ○	I ○	u ○

Go on.

12	f	F ○	y ○	B ○
13	T	k ○	t ○	M ○
14	g	o ○	G ○	j ○
15	S	q ○	A ○	s ○
16	h	Y ○	i ○	H ○
17	R	r ○	P ○	e ○

Go on.

18	i	R ○	V ○	I ○
19	Q	q ○	K ○	f ○
20	j	J ○	Z ○	b ○
21	P	d ○	S ○	p ○
22	k	g ○	K ○	T ○
23	O	M ○	o ○	a ○

Go on.

24	l	L ○	v ○	t ○
25	N	X ○	j ○	n ○
26	m	s ○	M ○	l ○
27	Z	z ○	D ○	C ○
28	A	h ○	L ○	a ○
29	y	Y ○	z ○	c ○

Go on.

30 B	I	P	b
	○	○	○
31 x	g	X	p
	○	○	○
32 C	c	H	F
	○	○	○
33 w	q	W	v
	○	○	○
34 D	J	d	a
	○	○	○
35 v	i	h	V
	○	○	○

Go on.

36	E	e ○	S ○	K ○
37	u	N ○	d ○	U ○
38	F	f ○	w ○	X ○
39	t	l ○	T ○	q ○
40	G	K ○	n ○	g ○
41	s	S ○	c ○	D ○

Go on.

42	H	Q ○	h ○	y ○
43	r	R ○	G ○	m ○
44	I	O ○	i ○	b ○
45	q	r ○	E ○	Q ○
46	J	V ○	j ○	z ○
47	p	g ○	f ○	P ○

Go on.

48	K	R ○	b ○	k ○
49	o	e ○	O ○	d ○
40	L	I ○	F ○	c ○
41	M	m ○	D ○	Z ○
42	n	N ○	x ○	A ○

Stop!

Name____

PART A: Matching Beginning Sounds Inventory

Sample 	 ○ ○ ○
1 	 ○ ○ ○
2 	 ○ ○ ○
3 	 ○ ○ ○
4 	 ○ ○ ○

PART A Matching Beginning Sounds Inventory

5	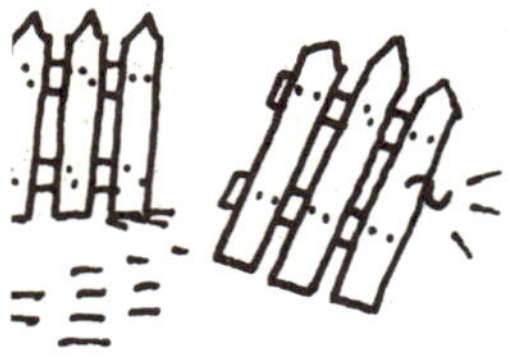			
6				
7				
8				

PART A Matching Beginning Sounds Inventory

9 			
10 			
11 			
12 			

PART A Matching Beginning Sounds Inventory

13

14

15

16

PART A Matching Beginning Sounds Inventory

17

18

19

20

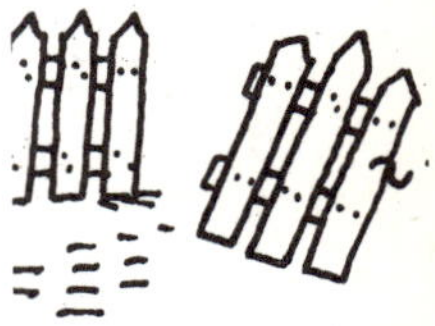

Name ____________________

PART B Matching Beginning Sounds Inventory

Sample 	
21 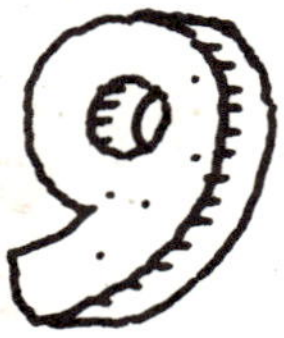	
22 	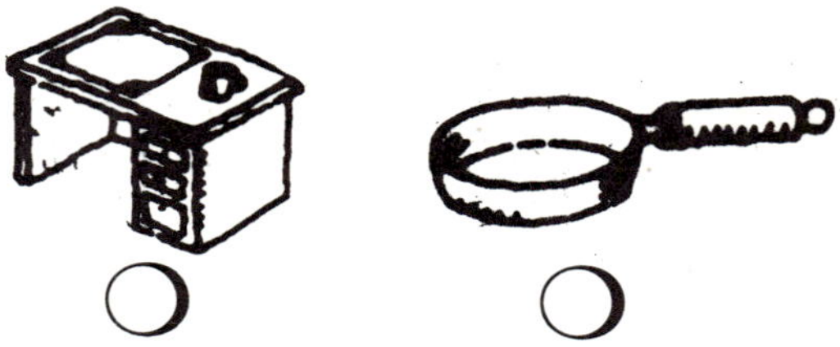
23 	
24 	

PART B Matching Beginning Sounds Inventory

25

26

27

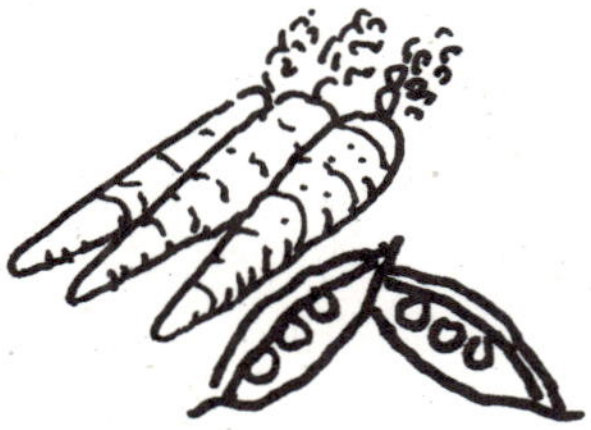

28

PART B Matching Beginning Sounds Inventory

29

30

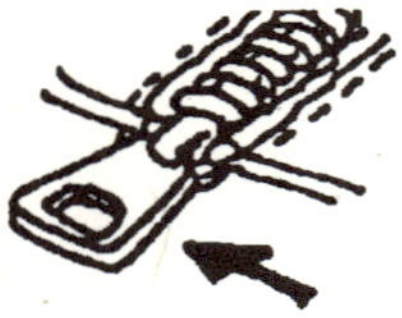

31

32

PART B Matching Beginning Sounds Inventory

33 

34 

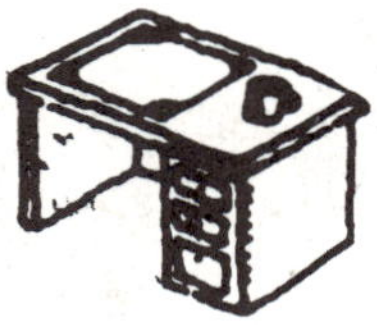  

35 

36 

PART B Matching Beginning Sounds Inventory

37 			
38 	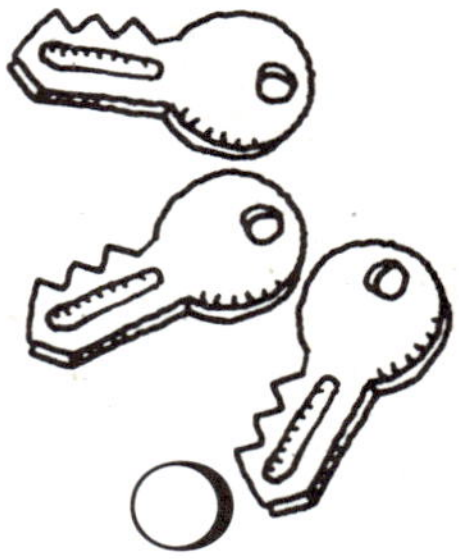		
39 			
40 			

Capital/Lowercase Letter Inventory

ANSWER KEY

1.	Z	27.	z
2.	A	28.	a
3.	y	29.	Y
4.	B	30.	b
5.	x	31.	X
6.	C	32.	c
7.	w	33.	W
8.	D	34.	d
9.	v	35.	V
10.	E	36.	e
11.	u	37.	U
12.	F	38.	f
13.	t	39.	T
14.	G	40.	g
15.	s	41.	S
16.	H	42.	h
17.	r	43.	R
18.	I	44.	i
19.	q	45.	Q
20.	J	46.	j
21.	p	47.	P
22.	K	48.	k
23.	o	49.	O
24.	L	50.	l
25.	n	51.	m
26.	M	52.	N

Matching Beginning Sounds Inventory

ANSWER KEY

Part A		Part B	
1.	bell	21.	necklace
2.	moon	22.	pan
3.	cup	23.	nail
4.	pie	24.	rake
5.	fox	25.	soap
6.	sock	26.	table
7.	heart	27.	vest
8.	book	28.	watch
9.	toothbrush	29.	yo-yo
10.	mouse	30.	zebra
11.	pencil	31.	ball
12.	balloon	32.	cage
13.	seal	33.	dog
14.	helicopter	34.	fork
15.	tiger	35.	girl
16.	car	36.	heart
17.	dog	37.	jet
18.	sun	38.	keys
19.	mop	39.	lock
20.	doll	40.	moon

"THE PERFORMANCE ASSESSMENT SHOULD BE USED JUST LIKE ANY OTHER CLASSROOM SHARED READING ACTIVITY."

Performance Assessment

INTRODUCTION TO PERFORMANCE ASSESSMENT

STORY: ***MR. FLOOP'S LUNCH***
Response activity, model papers

STORY: ***MY FRIEND WHALE***
Response activity, model papers

STORY: ***DINOSAUR FRIGHT***
Response activity, model papers

Introduction to Performance Assessment

The performance assessments are designed as benchmarks to help a teacher gauge each child's language development.

Like the emergent literacy inventories, these structured activities should not be seen as being more important than the ongoing observations you make while kid watching, conferencing with children about their portfolios, and so on. However, the activities do provide another opportunity to assess children's progress.

What are the benchmark assessments and when are they used?

Each of the three benchmark assessments consists of a story for shared reading, followed by a suggested written response. The first one can be used early in the school year after children are comfortable with the classroom routine. Use the second assessment early in the second half of the year, and the third near the end of the year.

How are the performance assessments administered?

By working with a group of six or seven children at a time, you can maximize your chances to observe what each of them can do. You can also help any children who may be anxious or uncertain about the task.

The performance assessment should be used just like any other shared reading activity:

1. Beforehand, build background and help children make predictions about story characters and events.

2. Do a shared reading with the children, pausing to let them discuss pictures and make predictions.

3. After reading, encourage several children to tell their reactions to the story. During the discussion, try to gauge children's level of participation. Are they contributing ideas? Do they seem to have a sense of story sequence? Can they interpret characters' feelings?

4. During the written response, encourage children to write about the pictures they are drawing. As children finish, have them tell you about their pictures, and ask them if you can write their ideas on the back. These comments will help you later as you evaluate their responses.

Mr. Floop's Lunch

by MATT NOVAK

On a day too beautiful to stay inside, Mr. Floop packed a delicious lunch and took it to the park.

When he found a nice spot, he opened his bag and took out a soft, warm roll. Mr. Floop loved rolls.

A bird perched on the bench.

"Would you like a bit of roll?" asked Mr. Floop, and he gave some crumbs to the bird...

and to all the other birds.

When the roll was gone, the birds flew away.

Mr. Floop reached into his bag again and pulled out a string of juicy sausages.

A small dog trotted over to the bench.

"I know what you want," said Mr. Floop, and he gave some sausage to the dog...

and to all the other dogs.

When the sausages were gone the dogs ran away.

Mr. Floop took some crunchy peanuts out of the bag.

A squirrel crawled down the branch of a tree. Mr. Floop fed a peanut to the squirrel...

and to all the other squirrels.

When the peanuts were gone the squirrels ran away.

Mr. Floop took a bottle of milk from his bag and poured himself a nice cool cupful.

A tiny kitten jumped onto the bench and purred very loudly. Mr. Floop looked at the kitten, and then he looked all around. There didn't seem to be any others. "Well," he said, "maybe just a little." And he gave some milk to the kitten...

and to all the other kittens.

When the milk was gone, the kittens ran away. Mr. Floop sighed. He'd given his bread to the birds, his sausages to the dogs, his peanuts to the squirrels, and his milk to the kittens.

He was very hungry.

Mr. Floop was still hungry when a woman came by carrying a picnic basket.

"Excuse me," she said. "May I sit here?"

"Please do," said Mr. Floop.

"Thank you," said the woman. "This is my favorite bench." She sat down next to him.

"Yes, it is nice," said Mr. Floop.

"I come here every day and share my lunch with the animals," she said. "I wonder where they are."

"I don't think they're hungry," said Mr. Floop.

"Really?" said the woman.

"Not anymore," he answered.

Then she saw Mr. Floop's empty bag. She smiled.

"Would you like to share my lunch?" she asked.

"I suppose I could eat a bite or two," Mr. Floop said.

"I don't like to eat alone," the woman said, and she handed Mr. Floop a soft, warm roll.

"Thank you," he said. "I love rolls."

"And I like sharing lunch."

Children's Responses to

Mr. Floop's Lunch

by Matt Novak

Suggested Response Activity: Have children draw and write about what might happen the next time Mr. Floop brings his lunch to the park.

Following are three model responses to the writing task above. They range from a "3" to a "1." A score of 3 can be thought of as "excellent" comprehension; a score of 2 can be thought of as "adequate"; and a score of 1 as "minimal" comprehension. Use these papers as anchor points as you weigh and balance different aspects of each of your children's responses.

SCORE: 3

This child makes a logical prediction for the story. He indicates that Mr. Floop will once again give his lunch away and will be sharing a lunch with the woman. The child's writing at the top of the picture indicates competence in the command of letters and letter/sound relationships. When asked what he had written, the child responded, "Mom and dad shared the rolls and said please." While the facts in the writing are not an exact match to the story, the child uses background knowledge and experience in his thinking.

SCORE: 2

The child demonstrates a reasonable prediction by drawing the pictures of the animals and Mr. Floop with his lunch bag, a picnic table (rather than a bench), and all four of the animals with whom Mr. Floop shared his lunch. This child seems to have an excellent understanding of the story. If he had attempted any labeling of the picture or writing about the picture, the score would have been 3.

SCORE: 1

The child's drawing is of a person with a smile. When asked about the picture, the child responded that it was Mr. Floop. The child did not seem to understand the idea of drawing what will happen the next time Mr. Floop brings his lunch to the park. The child does include his initials indicating some knowledge of letters and letter formation. However, the overall response is minimal and should be scored as a 1.

MY FRIEND WHALE

by Simon James

My friend Whale and I swim together every night.

My friend Whale is a blue whale.

My friend Whale makes the biggest splash of any sea creature, but he is a very slow and graceful swimmer.

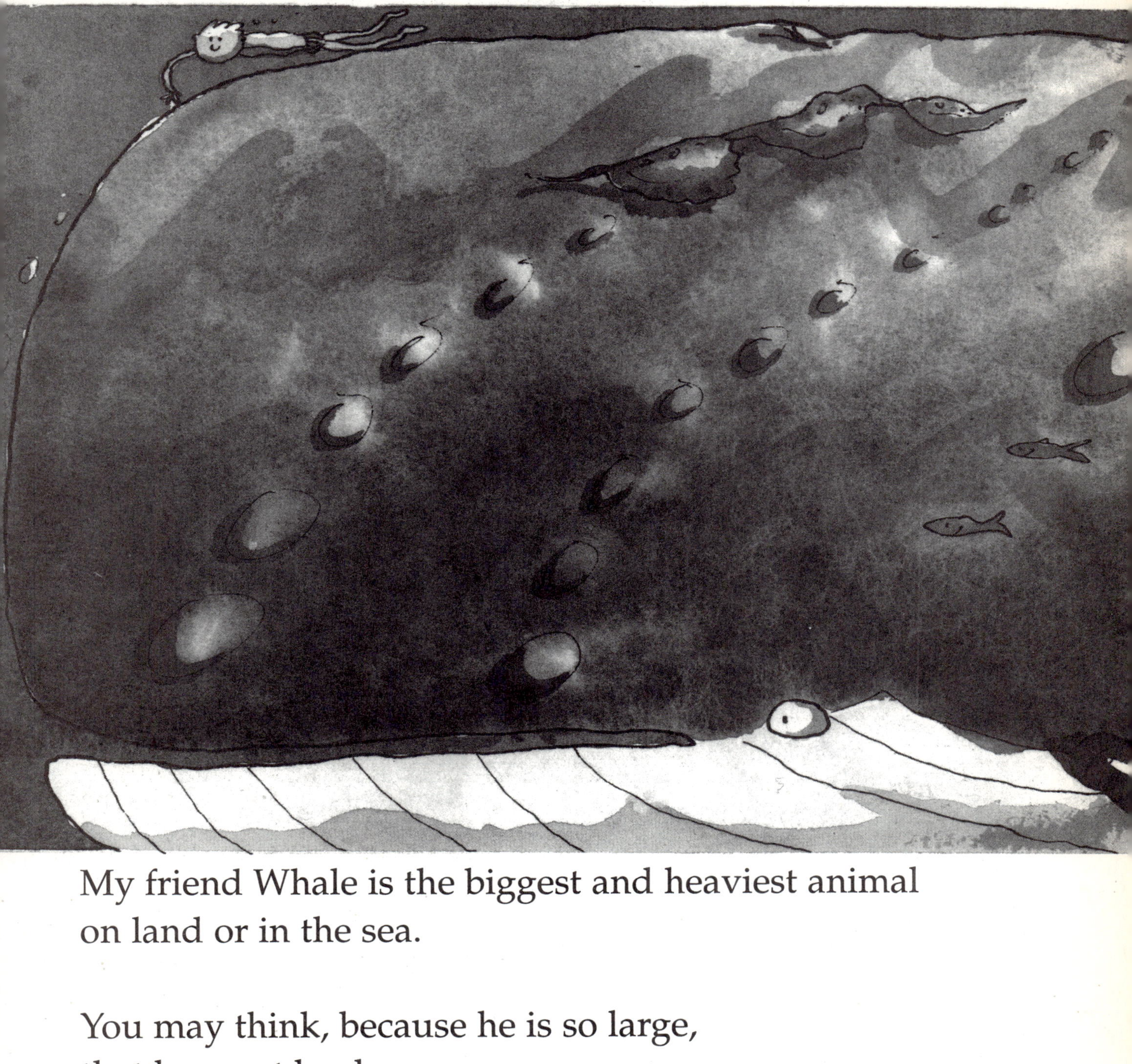

My friend Whale is the biggest and heaviest animal on land or in the sea.

You may think, because he is so large, that he must be dangerous.

But my friend Whale has no teeth.

In fact, he only eats fishy things smaller than my little finger.

My friend Whale can hold his breath underwater for almost an hour.

But because he is not a fish, he has to come up for air just like me.

My friend Whale can't smell anything.
My friend Whale can't taste anything.

But he has very good ears—
he can hear an underwater world of things that I can't.

My friend Whale speaks with squeaking, clicking, and whistling sounds.

Other whales can hear him from a hundred miles away.

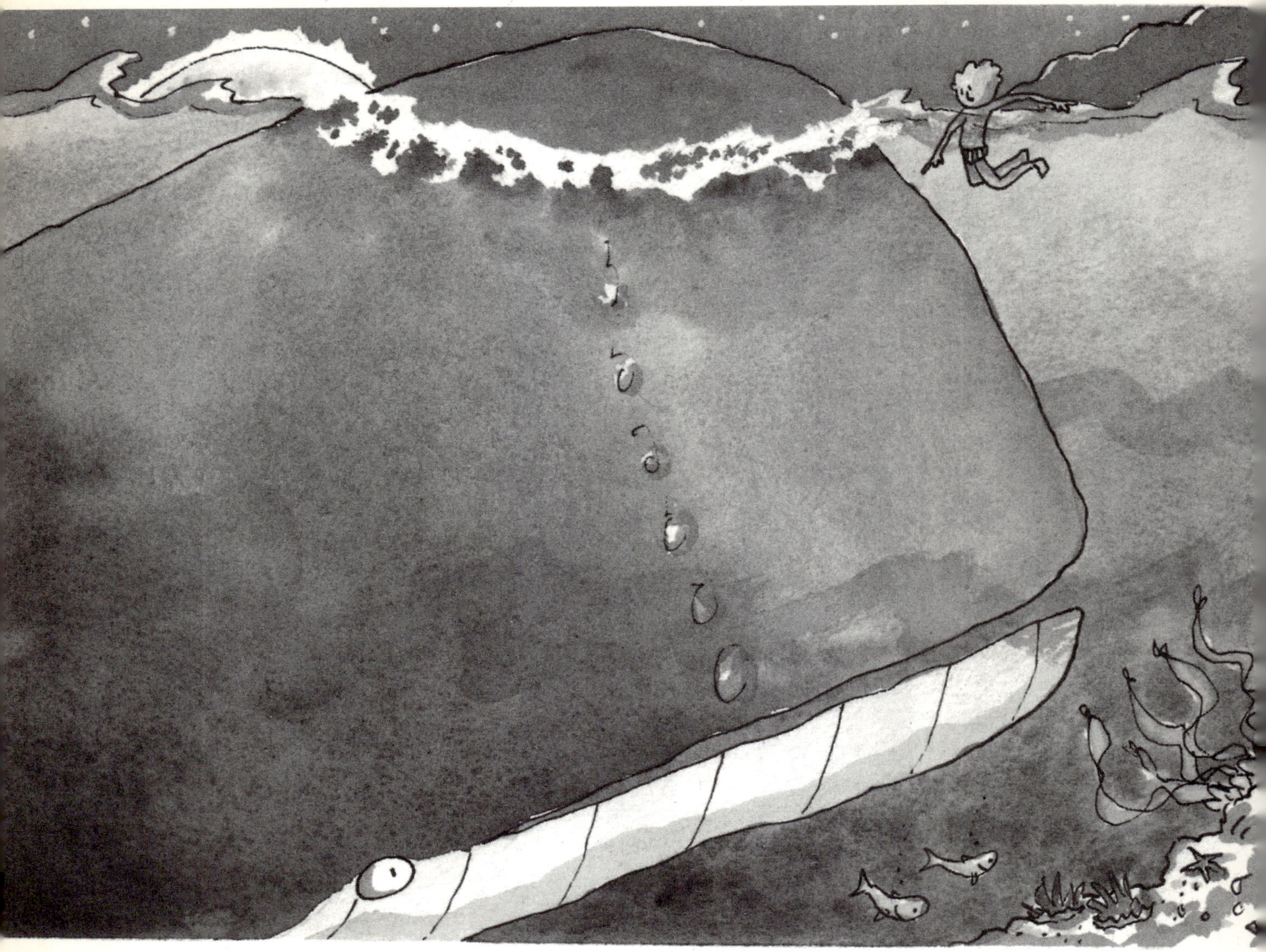

My friend Whale has very sensitive skin.
He can feel the slightest touch.

That is the way I say good-bye for the night.
See you tomorrow, my friend Whale.

My friend Whale really does make the biggest splash. But the next night, I don't see the spray of his spout or the splash of his tail.

He didn't come for me at all.

My friend Whale didn't come last night either,
or the night before.
Maybe he's found a new friend.

Or maybe something has happened to him.
Now my friend Whale only visits in my dreams.

Children's Responses to
My Friend Whale
by Simon James

Suggested Response Activity: Have children draw and write some new things they learned about whales that they want to tell a friend.

Following are three model responses to the writing task above. They range from a "3" to a "1." A score of 3 can be thought of as "excellent" comprehension; a score of 2 can be thought of as "adequate"; and a score of 1 as "minimal" comprehension. Use these papers as anchor points as you weigh and balance different aspects of each of your children's responses.

SCORE: 3

This child's picture and writing demonstrate an excellent understanding of the text and the task to write to her friend something new she learned about whales. The picture clearly shows the whale and the boy "riding" on it. The child writes that whales are graceful and they eat tiny fish. The command of letters and words is excellent. The emergent literacy skills of this child rate a score of 3.

SCORE: 2

The child demonstrates that he understood the task and the facts in the story. While not as sophisticated as the 3 model, the child does draw a picture of a whale. When the teacher asked what he had written about the whale, the child responded that he wrote "Whales can hear very well." It is not difficult to pick out the beginning development of sound/symbol relationships. However, this child has not yet developed a sense of the separation of groups of letters into words. The writing is at an adequate level for a child at this age.

SCORE: 1

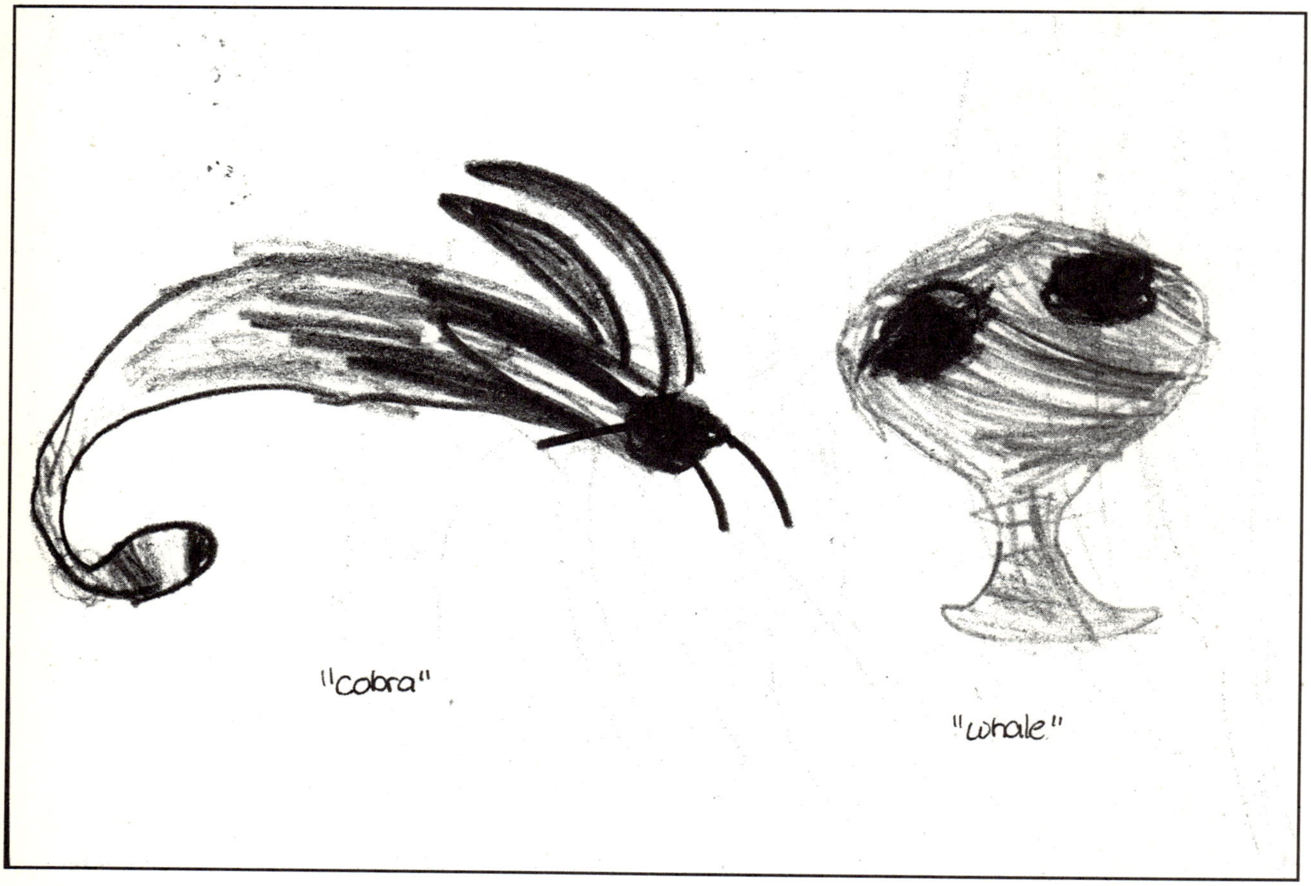

This child's drawing is not very comprehensible. When asked about the picture, the child said that he had drawn a whale and a cobra and said that the picture was about the story. It seems that the child did not comprehend the task and it is difficult to determine why he drew the cobra except that he may have been thinking about other animals. The child did not attempt any writing to explain the picture. The response is at a minimal level.

DINOSAUR FRIGHT

by Colin Threadgall

A long time ago, dinosaurs lived together in a forest by a lake.

One day there was a noise like thunder and the ground trembled . . .

THUMP! THUMP! THUMP!

It was a herd of giant Brachiosaurus.

"Go away!" cried the other dinosaurs.

But the Brachiosaurus only laughed as they crashed and bashed about.

They jumped into the lake and flooded everything with their enormous splashes.

They reared and stamped and bellowed.
"You go away," they boomed. "We like it here."

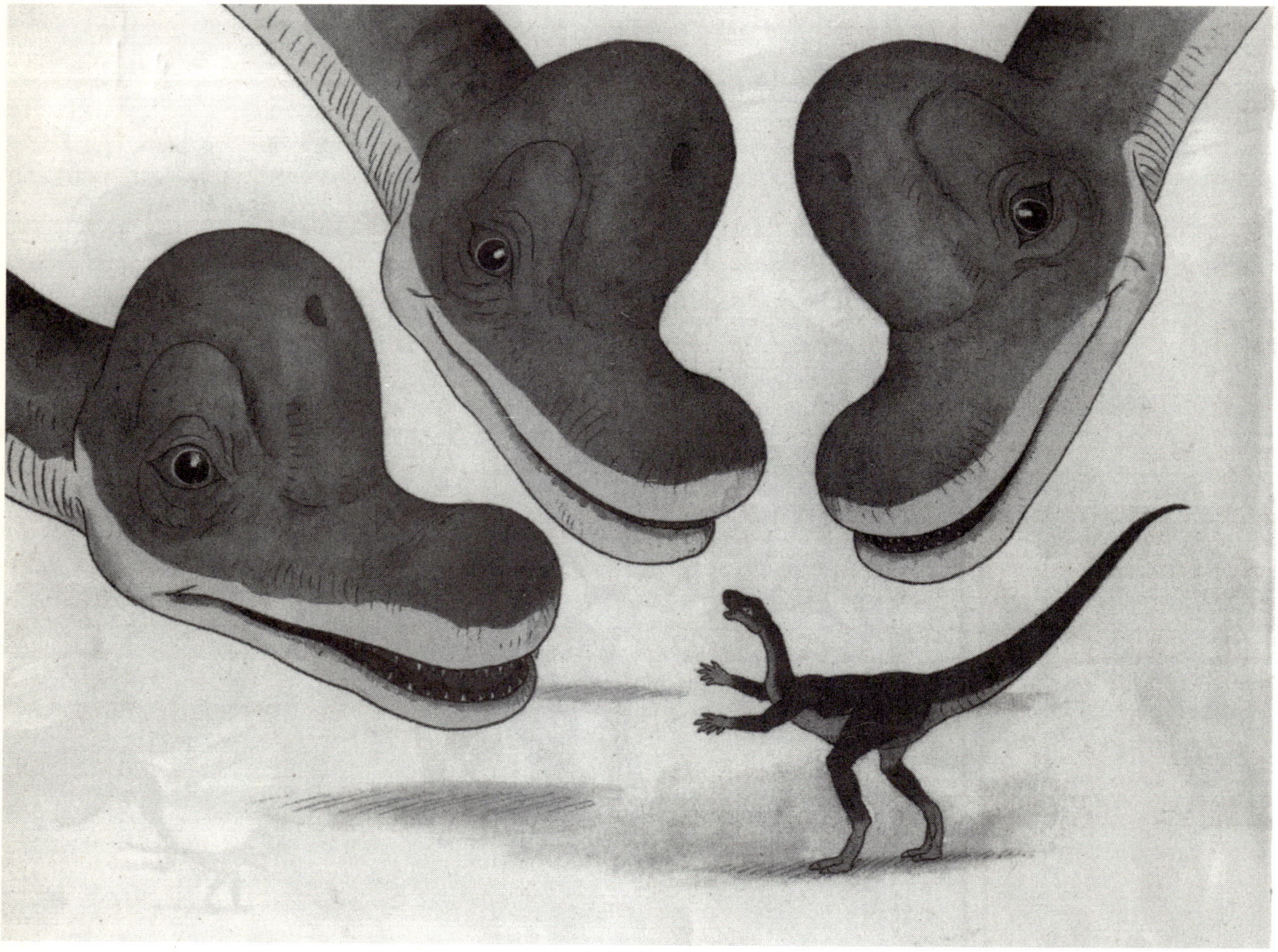

Little Nanosaurus crept up behind them.
"Beware," he said, "you might upset the monster."

"MONSTER!" roared the Brachiosaurus all together.
"We're bigger than any monster."

The other dinosaurs were puzzled.
"But there isn't any monster," they said.
"There will be tonight," said Nanosaurus.
He told them what to do. First they collected spiders' webs and stuck them on to the leafy tops of three fallen trees.

Then, when darkness fell, they caught as many fireflies as they could,

and stuck them on to the spiders' webs.

When it was truly dark they took the trees to the top of a hill.
Below them the Brachiosaurus lay sleeping.

The three trees were placed in position.
Then the dinosaurs howled and shrieked and roared and stamped and shook the trees. They made a dreadful noise.

The Brachiosaurus woke in fright. They saw a great fiery mouth and two enormous glowing eyes above them.

There was a monster! A huge monster!

Up they jumped and away they galumphed,
as fast as they possibly could.
And they never, never came back.

Children's Responses to *Dinosaur Fright* by Colin Threadgall

Suggested Response Activity: Draw and write about what frightened the big dinosaurs.

Following are three model responses to the writing task above. They range from a "3" to a "1." A score of 3 can be thought of as "excellent" comprehension; a score of 2 can be thought of as "adequate"; and a score of 1 as "minmal" comprehension. Use these papers as anchor points as you weigh and balance different aspects of each of your children's responses.

SCORE: 3

This child demonstrates an excellent understanding of the story. The "monster" in the mountain can be seen as the dinosaurs running away. The child uses imagination by showing the dinosaurs in tears, a logical response for a child who is frightened. The child wrote that it was the fireflies that scared the dinosaurs away. This is a logical conclusion since the light of the fireflies is what the dinosaurs saw. The picture and the writing together provide represent excellent comprehension. The writing indicates some command of letters and letter shapes and some awareness of capital letters.

SCORE: 2

The picture is not very clear as to what scares the dinosaurs. When asked about the three figures in the drawing, the child said that the first one is a child, the second is a monster, and the third is Batman. The child seems to have gone beyond the actual events in the story. The comprehension is somewhat confused, but it is clear the child understands the intent of the question. At the bottom of the picture, the child wrote "What scared the dinosaurs." When asked about the letters at the end of the line, the child responded that they said "The big monster mountain." The comprehension is reasonable, but the child is somewhat confused. The writing is not as mature as the 3 response. This response should be rated 2.

SCORE: 1

The child's drawing is of a dinosaur. When asked about the picture, the child said that the big dinosaurs ran away. There was no indication of an understanding of the task which was to show what scared the dinosaurs. The child knows the story was about dinosaurs, but the response does not show any further understanding. There is no attempt at writing. The response is minimal and should be scored 1.

Teacher Notes